This Thing in My Head

Jessica Aike

Jessica Aike is a British-Nigerian writer. Born in Lagos, Nigeria, Ms Aike relocated to London, England, at the age of two, where she was raised and currently resides.

She often jests that she came into the world with a pen and notebook in one hand, and a book in the other. A treasured recollection of her childhood is rooted in the various books she enjoyed reading, and since then the numerous fiction stories, stage plays and non-fiction pieces she has often spent her time writing. As her passion matured, she recognised an inner conviction directing her towards becoming a writer.

As a teenager, she began utilising various social media platforms to start often uncomfortable, but necessary conversations. Over the course of eleven years she has campaigned for a plethora of issues, with a special focus on the culture of silence surrounding the sexual, physical, and verbal abuse of children.

In 2020, she featured in an episode of Dr Bola Adebayo's podcast 'A Deep Look into the Issue of Rape', where she lent her voice to the growing conversation centred around sexual abuse, mental health, and emotional intelligence.

Her published work can be seen in **Afritondo, The Eyes of African Women, Literally Stories, Ariel Carter, Down in the Dirt Magazine, and Fiction on the Web, and Book of Matches** where she explores a range of themes. **This Thing in My Head** is her debut book.

CONTENTS

To my secondary school English teacher, I carry your words in my spirit. Thank you.

CULTURE

Culture teaches us to be seen and not heard. Culture tells us we know nothing and can bring nothing but child's play to the table. Culture demands that they steer the ship while shouting out orders, diminishing self-esteem, and demanding respect. But then arms get weary and visions get blurred. Then and only then does culture remember that the youths are the leaders of tomorrow. Then and only then does culture remember that knowledge does not solely lie in the arms of the elders. Then and only then does culture remember that life experiences are not a respecter of age. Then and only then does culture remember to plant healthy seeds in the young, so they in turn can pass on the baton.

If there is one thing culture quickly makes apparent, it is that children are solely a means to an end. Culture demands that wombs, loins, and seeds obey and multiply, not necessarily for genuine desire or structure or continuity. But because, how else does one showcase authentic masculinity and femininity if not by planting seeds they do not particularly care for. And in the event that those seeds do not sprout, culture serves ridicule. Culture is interesting: it ridicules those who cannot or will not procreate, only to turn around and encourage the abuse of the once-prized asset when the realisation that their trophy will one day grow, step out, and forge their own pathways. Culture demands you go and multiply; but should any harm come to that child, culture keeps quiet, becomes purposely obtuse. Culture says you are only a child, so know your place. But culture also enjoys the adultification of children. Science tells us a person's prefrontal cortex is not fully formed until twenty-five, but culture says, 'Adulting starts when I say it does.'

That is why when youngsters report abuse, culture asks the five-year-old child who stomached the unthinkable what they were wearing. Because culture likes to pick on the powerless, children are expected to quietly digest verbal abuse that would make the average adult crumble.

Culture says beating children, excessive tough love, and verbal abuse are rightful passages for everyone. They are to be romanticised, to be seen as a badge of honour. Culture says real men do not cry. Culture indoctrinates black women right from infancy to bear hardships and strive to seek and exude supernatural strength, even to their own detriment. Yet, somehow, culture displays shock when young boys cannot express themselves outside of the very anger they were told to cling to. Culture is in disarray when black women measure their worth by how much suffering they can endure. They have not been told that true strength embraces vulnerability. They have not been told that their gender, their race, does not automatically translate into assuming the role of a warrior. They have not been told that they too are allowed to rest.

A few years ago, there was online discourse about whether or not a person who has been sexually abused in the past should share it with their partner. One person said they should keep it to themselves, while most people said they would want their partner to tell them. Ultimately, the decision rests on the shoulders of the individual in question; but let us not forget how rape is viewed by many.

Culture says you are inadequate because you have been touched. Culture says you are damaged goods. Culture is family. Culture is friends. Culture tells you to keep mute because, what will people say? Culture tells you not to bring shame to this house. And when you fight back, it tells you you caused the rape. It tells you it was your fault.

With a culture that so readily points the finger at the ones who carry the burden, can we really be shocked to the core when people stomach the unthinkable and keep silent? With a culture that so readily upholds abuse, it is rather confusing when others are shocked that the same people who were indoctrinated with these ideologies go on to implement them in their own daily lives – ultimately recreating dysfunction. An apple does not fall far from a tree, so why are you surprised? What were you expecting? A culture that does not show and teach children empathy, cannot gasp in despair when they grow into monsters. This can be applied to beating children. When you beat a child out of love, as culture calls it, you are subconsciously training that child to believe love and violence are intertwined. Beating a child does not teach them to flee in the face of violence but, rather, to crave it, to think they are deserving of said abuse. And so, we have girls and women who bear the brunt to prove their value, and boys and men who remain in a quiet state of emotional turmoil, just ticking.

Beyond the emotional dysregulation and hushed psychopathy culture creates, culture also breeds people who fight for their right to suffer. Let us take Simone and Nancy. Simone and Nancy are having a conversation centred around childhoods and culture. As they converse, Simone gently touches on elements of her life. Nancy cannot relate to Simone's tumultuous childhood because Nancy has had a well-balanced childhood and life. But culture shows itself in its full glory, and now Nancy feels the need to prove she has in fact suffered more than Simone. When a culture prides itself on how much one can suffer, unnecessary competitions are birthed.

Just because something has been perpetuated for a long time, does not make it justifiable. It does not make it a thing that should be followed blindly. Clinging on to beliefs and practices that sprout nothing but chaos is madness.

May you not allow culture to create children who seek a home in the arms of strangers. May you not allow culture to forbid you from speaking positivity into the lives of your children. May you not refrain, in the name of culture, from telling and showing your children how valuable they are. May you remember that just as the average adult does not take kindly to mean spiritedness under the guise of critique, a child is also capable of sharing those same sentiments. May you not use your own hands to desecrate your seed, in the name of culture. Gone are the days when culture masks verbal abuse a tough love. Gone are the days when the beating down of a child's self-esteem is sold a prepping them for the real world. Honesty does not translate into bullying. A culture is as good as the people in it; and if we want a better culture, our focus should be on the children. Children have not yet been irredeemably hardened by life. Life has not yet diminished their nuances, nit-picked their self-confidence, or mocked their optimism. And if it has done that, children are still young enough to course-correct, to form healthier perspectives than those who came before them. They still have time to learn valuable skills as they navigate difficult spaces, to learn when to show their hand

and when to keep it concealed, when to lead with intellectual prowess, and when to lead with wisdom. They still have time.

BLACKNESS

As someone whose eclecticism bloomed as I grew, dibbling and dabbling out of different spheres came with the territory. Whether it was sitting comfortably in nerd culture before taking a stroll over to the Alté crew, or loving literature, enjoying a range of music, holding varied beliefs, and unwinding to classic Nollywood movies, being multifaceted was who I was and still am.

As I got older, I quickly learnt that not only was eclecticism shunned, but introversion was also demonised. Reserved personalities do not fit the stereotypes of the boisterous Nigerian, the loud black woman. It was a crime, met with constant ridicule, because how dare you show up as an authentic fully fledged human being, in a world that tells you you are a caricature. It is expected that you give people the performance of a lifetime, because what is blackness if not to perform, to posture, to dismiss nuance?

I raised children when I was a child and later worked with children as a young woman; but, of course, my campaign against the physical and verbal abuse of children equated to revoking my black card and ascribing to whiteness. Just as campaigning against the sexual abuse of little girls and little boys was hushed, dismissed, and assumed to be a rite of passage.

I believe respect is to be given regardless of a woman's marital and motherhood status. The looks I received from others however, told me everything I needed to know.

Freedom affords us rights to be, to practise religious beliefs in peace. I empathise with how constant chaos and a lack of stability can drive even the sanest of people into the arms of insanity. I also understand the dangers of religious fanaticism. I have watched people pray, cast, bind, tie, rebuke, and, of course, the 'die by fire' chants in the name of fixing the issues culture presents, yet nothing.

The outcome from my discourse has usually been disapproving glances. What was read as 'too liberal', 'too daring', was in actuality a push for more nuance, because with nuance comes rationale, balance, empathy. Ostracising is an interesting thing. You become familiar with what it is to dive for crumbs here and there, but never to receive the entirety of a thing. It is to stand as a partial outsider, not by your own desire, but by the decree of others.

Being black, being Nigerian does not mean accepting the entirety of your culture in order to prove a point. Just as there are elements of our culture that do not sit well with my spirit, there are elements that do. Like the richness of our proverbs. This is one of my favourites:

'Pesin character be like smoke wey dey inside bottle, even if you cover am las las e go escape'.

(People can pretend for only so long – it is just a matter of time before who they are at their core makes its way to the surface).

Or our regal attire. Or the fact that I am helplessly in love with yam porridge, a Nigerian dish that has wrapped me around its fingers for years. And, of course, the various beautiful cultural hairstyles. Just as we can walk and chew gum, two things existing at the same time, we can hold love and the encouragement to do better. Remember, you are a fully fledged human being, bloom.

SELF-ESTEEM AND PEOPLE-PLEASING

Who call im house dustbin no suppose vex wen im neighbour begin troway dirty for there.
(When you habitually treat yourself poorly, you should not be shocked to the core when others mirror your behaviour.)
Nigerian Proverb

We are often fed the dangerous rhetoric that encourages us to make room for toxic people, tolerate their excesses whilst wearing the saviour cape. The goal is to convince you that kindness translates into morphing between being a doormat and being Bob the Builder. You do not want to be perceived as the villain in anyone's story, so, you continue to look like bread, crumbling in the process whilst handing out loyalty to people who do not deserve it at all. Society also trains us to believe that having standards means you have a superiority complex.

Some of you have dealt with your own brokenness. Whether it was feelings of inadequacy, chronic people-pleasing, an inability to flee from detrimental co-dependent tendencies, and low self-esteem, you have been there. What separates you from your past brokenness is your dedication to doing the inner work. Talking about self-esteem, it is often assumed that the quality of a person's self-esteem is solely tied to what they look like – a notion I oppose. Self-esteem is not solely tied to how good someone looks. The quality of someone's self-esteem can also be measured by how well someone treats themselves, and what they tolerate from others.

I understand it is human nature to want acceptance and understanding, and I do not believe people should be shamed for their humanity, for their desires. We do ourselves a major disservice when we undermine just how great a human being's need for love is. I believe it is one of society's greatest minuses. I am also not against being affirmed by others, as wanting to be affirmed by others is not a bad thing; it is a human thing. However, there must be balance.

As a child, your self-esteem is built through your parents, your carers, your guardians, and so on. And in the event that you unfortunately did not get to experience the building of your self-esteem through your parents, carers, and guardians, you now become the starting point for you, eventually branching out to find your own symbiotic community. Having friends, mentors, and so on, who give you love, warmth, and encouragement is beautiful, important, and powerful, but as your grow, outsiders can only do so much. If the foundation of your acceptance and love does not stem from yourself, you will forever be at the mercy of others, because you cannot people-please your way into being respected. People can tell when you are love starved and willing to put up with the unthinkable in the name of attention; and if they are predatory, you run the risk of being abused.

I am sure some of you have been in situations where you have entertained someone you should have left at hello. Deep down you knew; you always knew. The truth constantly lingered in your subconscious, but you served it shady glances, dismissing the nagging feeling altogether. Maybe it was your pride, adamant that no one could ever play you; but the gag is, they did. Maybe it was your inability to see the bad in anyone that inevitably led you down this path. Regardless of your reasons, you entertained people who could never meet you halfway. You poured into them with such ease, whilst they hurriedly brought out their buckets and bottles, anxiously waiting to be filled to the brim, before eventually leaving and sending you into a state of despair. I have long grown weary of the 'You never know what you have until it's gone' anthem. In fact, I reject the notion. Sometimes people do know; they just do not believe you will stand up, put your heart back where it belongs and leave – until you actually do. Experience has taught me that sometimes, just sometimes, people are not as clueless as you think they are. Now, they have been contacting you recently. You message them at 10.00 a.m. and before you can say 'Jack Robinson', they have responded. In the past, it was you and only you who went above and beyond for people who did not reciprocate or appreciate your efforts. Now, they chase you down in a futile attempt to reel you back in with the faux love you no longer crave. No longer are you served half-heartedness.

When I peel back the layers, I realise the enemy is fear. People-pleasers often water down their needs and bury their true feelings and emotions because they do not want to offend the people in their life. You do not want to chase people away, so you keep mute at the expense of your own happiness. If more people were more upfront with others about what they wanted and what they would and would not tolerate, standards would be raised and time saved. You would live your life knowing the people in your life are the real deal, accepting you and all you encompass. And in the event that people leave, you understand that your authenticity is your natural filtering system. It filters out who should and should not be in your life. But the fear of not having the crowd surround you, even for a short while, cages you; it scares you into dishonesty. So, you pretend and tolerate the unthinkable. When you put out a false version of yourself, every person who comes into your life via your false persona is also a part of the illusion. In the end, you miss out on forming authentic connections because of fear and feelings of inadequacy, which is why I am an advocate of embracing solitude every now and then. Solitude gives room for introspection that cannot always be achieved when you are constantly around others, and, ultimately, clarity to identify other quality individuals you can surround yourself with. The key is to surround, not immerse. Solitude and introspection also teach you how important it is to form a habit of doing nice things for yourself (to the best of your ability). So, when you are in spaces with new people who are going above and beyond for you, you are still able to assess them through a clear lens and not a rose-tinted one. Being able to consistently meet the standards you set for yourself allows you to work out what you require from others and avoid throwing caution to the wind. Being appreciative of pleasant gestures is a good thing; I encourage it. However, until you are on solid ground with new people, your assessment cannot be biased. Oftentimes you are not who you attract – you are who you entertain.

May you understand that the onlookers you are worrying about do not have the power to bring you back to life when you die; so, do not give them that power now that you are living. May you no longer stumble and stutter in the face of rejecting half-heartedness from those who boldly lay their insatiable wants and needs at your doorstep yet encourage you to dismiss yours. May you learn how to assess the people in your life and put them into the right categories. Overestimating and underestimating your place in people's lives can wreak havoc. May you learn that self-respect is a powerhouse: it triggers growth and tells you to give to yourself first the love you so readily give to others.

BOUNDARIES

When you walk into a shop to buy a product worth £200, the likelihood of asking the shop owner to increase the price of the product is slim to none. Apply this to life. No one will increase your value. People will treat you as well as you treat yourself.

On this note, I want to bring attention to boundaries, standards, and background checks when it comes to exciting new people waltzing into our lives. Oftentimes, when a new person walks into someone's life, it is very easy to become so enamoured by them that your initial safety checks go out the window. Let us take Vanessa, for example. Vanessa grew up in a dysfunctional household where there were no boundaries or standards. Vanessa's chaotic world is a place where she can do as she pleases, treat people like trash, and still feel entitled not only to their forgiveness, but to the special place she has in their life. So here comes Vanessa the new person, striding into your life, and you become so enamoured by her entry, you throw caution to the wind and let her into your life.

Eventually, Vanessa does the unthinkable to you. You are stunned. She has done the worst and does not seem to care. You question your sanity and start to think that maybe, just maybe, you are overreacting.

I have learnt that sometimes it does not have to get bad before it gets better. Sometimes the disastrous results can be avoided if only we trust our judgements and leave certain people alone. Many people see the problematic traits, but think, 'No, they won't do that to me.' The idea that everyone you meet in life will automatically rid themselves of their problematic ways just because of you is not necessarily true. You have to show people what you will and will not tolerate, not just by your words but with your actions. Show Vanessa that in your space, your trust is sacred, and if respect cannot be given and boundaries cannot be honoured, then there is simply no room for her in your life.

People are not always going to tell you to enforce boundaries, because they benefit from your giving nature and your inability to say 'No'. They know you are selfless; they know you allow people to walk all over you; so, they habitually arrive at your doorstep clothed in their incessant demands for your help. Behaving as if they will not survive if you do not help them. But what no one ever tells you is, they survive. They always do. I often watch people writhe in their misery as they chant the 'Nice guys finish last!' anthem. I say, yes, nice people do finish last, but kind people with boundaries do not. Narratives that encourage kindness even to the detriment of yourself worry me. They reiterate the warped concept that you cannot be happy, or kind, or in love without somehow being a doormat in the name of kindness and selflessness. If I asked you to fill my cup with an empty jar, you would question my sanity; yet that is how your inner self feels when you consistently stretch yourself thin even when you have nothing to give. I often ponder if the issue at hand is merely an inability to be unkind to people or is, rather, a saviour complex.

Kindness with boundaries differs from nice-people syndrome. Kindness is rooted in security; kindness has limits; kindness says 'No'. Nice-people syndrome on the other hand is rooted in insecurity and entails constant people-pleasing.

Nice-people syndrome does not give room for you to reflect deeply on how best to handle situations. Neither does it give room for one to leave comfortably. Instead, it forces people to stay with people they do not want to be with out of obligation, not because they genuinely want to. It also encourages the fast-forgiveness culture and the endless chances and unconditional-love notion, concepts that I do not believe in.

People want to have their cake and eat it too; so, when your actions show them 'No', it unsettles them. They do not expect it, because the average person does not address foolishness straight away; they sit around hoping things will get better. But very rarely do things magically become better. And so, I want more people to learn to enforce boundaries with others right from the beginning, because your fear of being labelled as rude and stuck up can potentially burn you in the end. People know boundaries are a powerhouse, which is why you are met with resistance when you introduce them into your life. Boundaries mean you will no longer allow problematic behaviour to grow comfortable in your presence, in your space, in your life, and that unsettles some people. Boundaries are one hell of a filtering system; so, when you see people throwing tantrums because they can no longer serve you half-heartedness and get away with it, make a mental note of it and ensure that whoever it is you allow into your life exudes quality.

Sometimes, choose self-preservation. Sometimes, save yourself before you hurriedly run off to save others. Sometimes, save yourself, so when you render help to people, you no longer operate as a broken person but as a whole individual. Helping people is not the enemy; indulging in self-destruction in the name of help is. It would be great if more people respected your wishes from the get-go; but, unfortunately, not everyone can be reasoned with. Parameters. Limits. Aim for diplomacy and politeness when it is safe to do so. Kindness with boundaries. Learn to nip things in the bud early on. May you learn to find the sweet spot between selfishness and selflessness. One must learn the art of saying a firm 'No' and taking care of self-become-stretching on forever for others.

FAMILY

People are often told to flee from problematic romantic relationships and friendships, but what no one ever seems to explore is the genesis of the problem. Why are people tolerating abuse? Who told them that suffering is an extension of love? Upon closer inspection, you realise that almost everything starts in the home, yet on so many occasions people are encouraged to surround themselves with the very people that have been instrumental in the dysfunction.

I will be the first to admit that healthy family relationships are important, but the operating word here is healthy. The 'family is everything' notion tells you to embrace the family members who abuse you. It does not tell you to forgive for your sanity, for your peace of mind, for your quality of life. It does not tell you to work through your issues at a steady pace. Encouraging you to work through your feelings and work towards closure for yourself is never once brought up, but pressurising you to overlook the trauma you suffered at the hands of your family is consistently shoved in your face. Forgiveness does not always automatically translate into reconciliation. Sometimes you can work things out with people. Sometimes you can forgive and reconcile. And sometimes all you can give is forgiveness – with a firmly closed door.

Over the years, all in the name of 'family is everything', I have watched people become shadows of themselves, suffering at the hands of the people who should be in the sufferer's corner. Conversations centred around boundaries usually point to manipulation being a key tool used to trigger feelings of guilt within people who come from toxic families and want to keep their distance. Many people were taught from young that family is everything; so, in turn, they internalise this rhetoric and struggle with freeing themselves from the shame and guilt that comes with it. I have a question: If someone were to treat you the way your family members do, how would you respond? Yes, family is important. But no, family cannot be everything in the face of habitual abuse. Healthy boundaries do not make you a bad person. Sometimes you can reconcile and move on, and sometimes you cannot reconcile, and that is OK.

It is also important to break the notion that coming from a two-parent household automatically translates into someone 'having it easy'. The number of parents involved does not override the quality required in raising decent children. Sometimes two does not always equate to better. There are people who struggle with childhood trauma who come from two-parent households, people who often feel like they have no grounds to complain because they somehow had it 'easier than others'. I ask, though, how do you compare pain to pain? Are pain and struggle competitors? If children who come from both single- and two-parent households are capable of being victims of traumatic childhoods, our focus should be on the quality of parenting, and not just on how many parents are involved. I thoroughly understand that parenting is not a walk in the park; but, from all the horror stories we have heard over the years, do you not think we can do better?

FRIENDSHIPS

Oftentimes we ask for people who will turn up for us in our down times, because life can sometimes feel like we are being served more chaos than peace. So, wanting a support system during the dark times is understandable and natural. But what we sometimes forget to ask for are people who can genuinely celebrate us when our lives start to light up. What happens when we stop crawling and start walking? Are our down-times people capable of handling our up season?

As someone who has constantly opened herself to evolving, I now understand that, just because my growth looks good, does not automatically mean that those who cling so closely will also partake in my joy. Experience has taught me that it is 'Cheers to growth!' until that growth encompasses making healthy new friendships; and now it's suddenly,

'No new friends; I ride only with my day ones.'

I have never really understood the concept of encouraging people to grow, make better decisions when it comes to whom they allow in their life, and then turning around to castigate them when they go on to make healthy new friendships. There is something about people forging healthy connections and relationships that unsettles some, ruffles feathers, causes quiet chaos.

So, as long as your growth is not harming anyone, please do not minimise how far you have come for those who demand closeness but embody hatred. Please, do not resist growth when it brings genuine people to your doorstep – just because you have not known them for fifty-five years. Otherwise, you will find yourself, because of throwbacks, in a chokehold with friendships you are supposed to leave behind. It is about the consistency of their good character, not solely about the number of years you have known them. Genuine friendships should allow room for growth. They do not stifle you. They do not castigate you as you evolve, frequently shoving you back into their tightly monitored box, reminding you of who you were in childhood or at seventeen or somewhere in adulthood, trying to work things out.

One thing I have learned is that people tend to believe that if people harbour ill towards them, those foes will make this clear. I used to believe this too, but over the past few years I have realised that this is not always the case. I have come to understand how important it is to cut yourself loose with your own hands, because people will keep you around for their own selfish gain as they waste your time and serve you the bare minimum. There are a plethora of reasons why people will keep you around, but two of the most common are, 'I do not want you, but I do not want anyone else to have you' and 'I want to keep enjoying the benefits of having you around without having to give anything back.' You are not supposed to be treated like a cash machine only to be acknowledged to satisfy their greed. You pour into people, but nobody pours into you. You appreciate the quirks and uniqueness of people, but nobody appreciates your quirks and uniqueness. You pour out so much love, care, and support, yet get nothing back. Experience has shown me that most people usually make friends at the level of their own self-esteem, which is why I encourage you to do the inner work so you can release yourself from the chokehold of toxic friendships, and open yourself to symbiotic platonic relationships.

I understand the grief and awkwardness that accompany the ending of a close friendship. Manoeuvring through your feelings and confronting loneliness is never easy, no matter how you spin it; but the ability to let go and move forward is a key skill to possess. Old friends are what they are: the past. Deciding to live in pretence for the sake of peace is counterproductive. You can simmer down how much you have outgrown people for only so long. Sooner or later, the growth you so desperately try to water down will show itself. So, here you are – stagnant, because the loyalty you give people is stronger than the loyalty you give yourself.

ROMANCE

We cannot and should not subdue the human need for love, because wanting to love and be loved back is not a bad thing. But what we should be doing is ensuring that people are empowered with self-love, self-respect, self-awareness, and self-esteem so they do not lose themselves completely in the name of love. We should not be shaming people because they want love; rather, we should be giving them the tools to navigate those waters.

A common theme I often hear in the dating world is vetting. I believe in vetting. I understand the premise behind vetting, assessing one's character and pacing. I also understand that you can only assess others at the level of your own self-esteem. Someone could vet another person for six months straight, but if the person doing the vetting has low self-esteem, with loneliness being their biggest motivator, they will see nothing but stars. I often encourage people not to get so caught up in a person's public etiquette, that they forget to pay attention to the rest of that person's character.

An older divorcee once shared her divorce story. Her ex-spouse was the boss of chivalry. They were admired by many, with other couples often wishing their partners would emulate their behaviour. Sounds great, right? Well, it turns out it was all for show. Underneath his chivalry, he was physically and mentally abusive, and a frequent cheater.

A shaky sense of self believes that sex, 100-carat rings, weddings, marriages, and children are magic potions that instantly wash away someone's problematic ways. Turning yourself into a flexible ruler during sex is not a guarantee that someone will change for the better. Swinging in the air (if you like it, I love it) during sex is not a guarantee that someone will change for the better. Proposals are not a guarantee that someone will change for the better. Having children is not a guarantee that someone will change for the better. Yes, having a child can influence someone into being responsible, but that does not mean they love, respect, or care for you. Yes, people can become better people in healthy environments. Yes, people can change with support systems in place, but the change fundamentally stems from them. You cannot use sex, weddings, and children as tools to force someone into becoming the version you want them to be. Please put your tools away: you are not Bob the Builder. Some people fail to understand that people will ultimately do whatever they want to.

A shaky sense of self also downplays the importance of shared core values in long-term relationships, opting to only cling to shared hobbies. Am I saying that having things in common interests with a romantic partner is inconsequential? No. What I am saying is that for those who require depth and longevity, being equally yoked is critical and transcends hobbies. Experience is an interesting teacher: it teaches you that sometimes, just sometimes, you can have the same hobbies as someone whilst having vastly different core beliefs.

Low self-esteem also fuels the notion that the beauty of romantic relationships is rooted in the long-suffering participants being rewarded for their apparent bravery. This is a long-standing belief held by many; it is also a belief I oppose. It is why we have got to a stage in society where cheating has become so glamorised – the standard for a healthy relationship now boils down to 'Do they cheat? No? Great, let's date.'

Are you aware that there are people who have very poor communication skills? Are you aware that you can spend your last breath telling someone how you want to be treated, and they still will not comprehend anything you have said? Remember, communication does not equate to comprehension. How about the people who are incredibly dismissive? Your partner comes to you in an emotional state needing your support and advice, but because loyalty is the only thing that seems to matter, you completely dismiss them. I almost forgot, you do not cheat; so, nothing else is required from you. Please do not misconstrue my words. I am by no means downplaying the importance of fidelity. All I am saying is, regardless of the state we get to as a society, the health and functionality of romantic relationships should transcend one's ability to be loyal. Quality does not solely boil down to one thing; quality is multifaceted. I want more people to prioritise self-development, to go where they are truly embraced and cherished, and thoroughly understand that you cannot force anyone to become better.

Last but not least, dear everyone, if you are getting to know someone romantically, or you are in the early stages of a relationship, and they keep going on and on about how much they want to impregnate you, or how much they want to get pregnant for you, it may just be a trap. So yes, vet, assess, and pace, but also remember to be honest with yourself about where you are on the self-esteem scale.

I have never claimed to be a relationship guru, and you do not have to listen to me, but I do like to make notes on what I have seen so far in life. As you manoeuvre through life, meeting different people, may you lead with a healthy self-esteem.

ENVY

They say some people are more predisposed to envy than others, so maybe I won the genetic lottery. You may assume I am being cocky, lying, or am ill-equipped to speak on this issue, as it is not a pressing issue of mine; still, I ask that you walk with me.

Social media has its advantages and disadvantages. I have experienced both the good and the bad. One word that often accompanies social media is comparison. For as long as I can remember, I have always been of the understanding that in life there will always be someone in a much better standing than you; the only difference is you are now seeing it everywhere, unlike before the social media era. Let us take an attractive person for example. Unless you decide to physically assault the individual in question, which I strongly advise against, your envy and feelings of inadequacy are not going to change what they look like. The same thing applies to successful people. Sure, you can find different ways to slow down someone's journey to success, but you cannot stop their destiny. So, what gives?

I believe that envy and animosity are usually a sign of a lack of contentment and appreciation of self. There are women in the world who look better than me, have better lives, and will always be steps ahead. But that does not mean I am not worthy, or attractive, or successful in my own right; it simply means we are playing in different fields. Do I really want to live my life in complete disarray because someone looks better or has achieved things I have not? No, I do not.

It is important to remember that there are individuals who have worked very hard for extended periods of time before starting to reap their successes. Pangs of envy are not a cause for alarm, but deep-rooted envy becomes dangerous if it morphs into calculated, meticulous sabotage. This behaviour screams that you need to go back to the drawing board to assess your emotions. It is also important to consider the distress you bring to the doorstep of the individual, due to your envy and feelings of inadequacy, when you make your insecurities their problem. As I have grown, one thing has become apparent to me: our insecurities are our own, and nobody has to put up with being projected on to. Instead of trying to control how others live their life, monitoring what they do and looking for loopholes to dissect, breakdown, and destroy, you could be developing a better sense of self. You could be on your self-actualising journey, learning your triggers, going back to the drawing board, assessing if your confidence is actually intact, and ensuring the confidence you portray is secure.

For as long as we live, beauty and success will always be celebrated. One could argue that the metrics we use to define success should be readjusted, that in the world of beauty, diversity should be our main goal. But, before we reap the benefits of those said changes, we live in the now. I encourage self-actualisation, self-mastery, and contentment.

During some of my darkest moments, my mind pondered on a particular woman who truly inspired and still inspires me. I thought about her successes and how hard she must have worked to reach where she is. I would say to myself,

'She also went through some difficult moments and overcame them. If she was able to pull herself up, I think I may just have a fighting chance. We may not have the same resources, but I am inspired. I want to see what happens if I refuse to give up on myself'. What I am saying in essence is, you decide how you channel other people's success. Sometimes people pressurise others intentionally. Sometimes people intentionally make others feel less than they are; but sometimes, just sometimes, no one is pressurising you, and blaming innocent people for your feelings of inadequacy will not get you to where you want to be or build a healthy self-esteem.

WELCOME TO MY WORLD

As a child, I often told myself that when the opportunity presented itself, I would grab it with both hands, immersing myself in the world of self-mastery, self-actualisation, and, most importantly, of freedom. That opportunity came in the package of education when I was a teenager far from where I was raised and, as I had promised myself, I grabbed it.

I have always been a quiet and introverted person and, as a survivor of bullying, have also experienced social anxiety. While being on my self-mastery and self-actualisation journey, I have noticed that my social anxiety has decreased, while my introverted, and quiet nature have stood, unflinching. I now know which of my personality traits are organic and which have been formed through pain and trauma. The past few years have been dedicated to altering my lens, developing emotional intelligence, because what is intellectual prowess without emotional intelligence? And last, but certainly not least, coming home and being at peace with my own womanhood.

I have been a tomboy my whole life, and to a certain extent still am. It is not an act, a costume I put on and take off, but an organic part of my personality. In saying that, however, I also recognise how trauma can exaggerate elements of our personality. I cannot speak for other people, but beyond the attire, sports activities, and mannerisms, my tomboyish nature has housed a ticking hostility. As a child I often felt that the tougher and rougher I appeared to be, the fewer problems I would have to deal with. Which, on one hand, sounds great, but this thing called life is not binary. It is not static, nor black and white. Things do not always sit nicely in boxes. Sometimes life is messy, nuanced. Sometimes there are numerous shades of grey and sometimes there is colour. What I am saying in essence is, having a singular attitude and response in the name of protection does not always serve you.

The thing about trauma is, it creates the 'That is just how I am' illusion, which leads to people embracing a brokenness they assume is their authentic self. It does not give them room for pause, for reflection. Yes, there will always be elements of your personality that are organic, but when you have dealt with life's tragedies, the likelihood of having a fragmented personality, an altered sense of self, almost becomes inevitable. People often cling to their pain and trauma because that is all they know. My question is, who are you outside your trauma, outside your pain?

Throughout my life I have always been seen as the 'mature one', with my age often being questioned. To that I say, experience teaches you that tragedy is not a respecter of age, nor does it look at your face when it bursts through your doors – you are simply expected to buckle up. So, when you have carried the weight of a maturity honed in your infant years, you develop such an intense relationship with responsibility that you forget to stop, to breathe, to live.

When I decided to ease my way out of survival mode, one of the changes that became apparent to me was my femininity and how at ease we are. Seeking and embracing balance, slowing down the tempo, and being present in the moment remain game changers in my world.

Amidst the sunshine and rainbows, it is important to note that sometimes self-mastery and self-actualisation are not always met with joy. Sometimes they come with scrutiny, because for some people, declaring the unworthiness of others soothes their ego. Throughout my life I have encountered people who clamour to squash me into their ideals, their boxes, in an attempt seemingly to make sense of me but, ultimately, to control me. They usually fail. Talking about control, a few years ago a friend of mine said that people who seek to control others often lack control in their own lives.

My friend sees control, I see fear. Fear of people who seemingly take up too much space, just by being themselves. It is why people intentionally dismiss the multifarious nature of a person, because how can you control what you cannot pinpoint? Binary thinking and pushing the notion that one-dimensional people should always be mirrored can be dangerous. Just as life leans more towards the greys than the blacks and whites, people should also be able to be themselves, to float, in peace. I march to the beat of my own drum because it is in my authenticity that I find my true peace and confidence. The next time you want to project on to others, to control them, remember that they are not your enemy. Fear is.

Beyond the heavy subjects I explore in the pieces I write, you can find me somewhere, living. Maybe I am unwinding with cranberry juice in a wine glass, or I am dressed for dinner. Sometimes I am at the nail salon, and other times I am in nature. I am living. I understand some people will poke holes in my identity, because how can I serve brain power on Monday only to get giddy over freshly manicured nails on Sunday? I recognise these people are not my people. To leave a mark, my mark, on the world, to tell stories that matter, whilst honouring what womanhood means to me, is all I am after.

May I continue to learn when to advocate, and when to embrace stillness. May I continue to learn when to show my hand, and when to keep it concealed. May I continue to learn when to be stoic, and when to be soft and warm. May I continue to find the sweet spot between selfishness and selflessness, because, yes, selfishness is good sometimes. May I continue to learn when to be empathetic and understanding, and when to set firm boundaries. May I continue to learn that, yes, you can be passionate about certain social ills; but, no, you do not always have to wear your politics. May I continue to learn. Cheers to balance, to nuance, and to introspection.

MISCELLANEOUS

Can we really claim to be humble if we have not yet reached where we want to be? Isn't true humility measured by acquiring what you want, without drastically morphing into a monster?

Sometimes, we get so caught up in our day-to-day activities and problems that we forget to congratulate ourselves on how far we have come and practise gratitude. Life is fleeting – enjoy it whilst you are here

People are multifaceted. People are layered. People are not one way. Please give them the room and understanding to grow. Allow them to be, to show themselves in their entirety instead of putting them in a box.

I have come to understand that just because you have forgiven someone and moved forward with your life, does not mean their conscience is at rest. Some people struggle with the change that accompanies forgiveness. Yes, I forgive you, but things are naturally going to be different from now on, which can be hard for some to stomach.

When you are passionate about succeeding in your craft, dedicating yourself to your craft is not the only important thing you must do. You must also learn to surround yourself with people who are truly doing the work to get to where they want to be. You must differentiate between the hard work shown through actions and the hard work that only falls from someone's lips. The latter, though common, is futile. Iron sharpens iron and if you are the only one with the sharpener, who exactly is sharpening your iron as you are busy running around trying to sharpen the iron of others?

Introspection allows you to put your ego aside and assess situations. Sometimes it is the other person's fault, sometimes it is no one's fault, sometimes it is everyone's fault, and sometimes it is you. The aim is not to turn yourself into a martyr constantly taking the blame for others, but to get into a habit of practising self-reflection. I have learned that nothing in my space changes for the better unless I am proactive about it. Introspection creates the space for change; egos encourage stagnancy. It is very soothing to scream 'Yassss' and click fingers when the message is not about holding the mirror to your own issues; but sometimes holding the mirror to yourself is necessary for growth. Please, do not miss out on growth because your ego wants to take centre stage.

Sometimes we become so blinded by the what ifs, that we miss out on the certainties of life.

CLOSING REMARKS

I did not write this book as a know it all or a life guru, I wrote this book as a 20 something year old young woman, who has seen so much so soon so young. In other words, my young life has held quite a number of secondary and primary experiences that have taught me a lot about the world. I wrote this book because I wanted to share what was in my head, to have a concrete place that held many of my varied beliefs, and of course, to encourage empowerment for those who need it.

As someone who came into the world with a notebook and pen in one hand, and a book in the other, I think it is safe to say that I have been an avid fiction reader from the moment I could breathe. I would like to think that my years of reading has enabled me to find the sweet spot, to write a book that embraces and incorporates the various shades of grey.

Society has a habit of feeding us dishonesty; a dishonesty that you discover through primary and/or secondary experiences. Sometimes, people are able to learn the ropes and figure out a game plan early on, while for others, they learn after a series of hardship and horror.

It is important that I am honest with you. I do not want my book to mirror the typical self-help book that sells you hopes and dreams, speaks in absolutes, and lacks perspective-taking. I want to lead with understanding, nuance, and compassion. I also want to lead with the importance of empowering oneself, (especially the youth) introspection, personal responsibility, course correcting, and healthy adulting that shows in ones character and behaviour. Yes to honouring and respecting the numerous shades of grey, but also yes to getting your life together and understanding how the world works.

If I could do anything in this world, it would be to end poverty and child abuse. Unfortunately, I do not have such power. I know I cannot save the world and I am under no delusion that I can. But what I have is my mind, my thoughts, my pen, my words. I can only hope that the work I have done throughout the years is enough to create a dent, enough to leave a mark, a mark that questions, and makes life easier for the ones that are coming after us.

This Thing in My Head